WASHINGTON

CHRISTINE WEBSTER

Consultants

MELISSA N. MATUSEVICH, PH.D.

Curriculum and Instruction Specialist
Blacksburg, Virginia

TERESA BATEMAN, M.L.I.S.

Librarian
Brigadoon Elementary
Federal Way, Washington

JENNIFER MEYER

Youth Services Librarian
Spokane Public Library
Spokane, Washington

CHILDREN'S PRESS®

AN IMPRINT OF SCHOLASTIC INC.

New York • Toronto • London • Auckland • Sydney • Mexico City
New Delhi • Hong Kong • Danbury, Connecticut

Washington is in the northwestern part of the United States. It is bordered by Idaho; Oregon; British Columbia, Canada; and the Pacific Ocean.

The photograph on the front cover shows Mount Shuksan in the Cascade Range.

Project Editor: Meredith DeSousa
Art Director: Marie O'Neill
Photo Researcher: Marybeth Kavanagh
Design: Robin West, Ox and Company, Inc.
Page 6 map and recipe art: Susan Hunt Yule
All other maps: XNR Productions, Inc.

Library of Congress Cataloging-in-Publication Data

Webster, Christine.
   Washington / by Christine Webster.
     p. cm. -- (From sea to shining sea)
Includes bibliographical references and index.
   ISBN-13: 971-0-531-20817-5
   ISBN-10: 0-531-20817-6
   1. Washington (State)--Juvenile literature. I. Title. II. Series.
   F891.3.W43 2008
   979.7--dc22   2007047603

TABLE of CONTENTS

CHAPTER ONE

INTRODUCING THE EVERGREEN STATE

A hiker stands next to a huge Douglas fir tree in Olympic National Park.

Washington is an extraordinary state. It is the only state in the Pacific Northwest that has both a rain forest and a desert. It has magnificent coastal beaches, dense rain forests, and glacier-covered mountain peaks. You can even gaze into an active volcano. All this in one state!

Washington wasn't always a state. At one time Washington was part of the Oregon Territory. Famous explorers Meriwether Lewis and William Clark led an expedition to the Pacific Northwest in 1805. Washington was one of the places they reached and opened up for other settlers. In the years following, many people traveled thousands of miles to make their homes in the new territory.

Just as it was in the early days, Washington today is heavily wooded. More than half the state is covered in forests, which is how it earned the nickname the Evergreen State. Evergreen trees stay green all year long. They grow mostly in Washington's western and northeastern regions. Washington is also noted for its rain, which mostly falls in the western part of the state. Thanks to the moist climate, trees such as the Douglas fir grow to enormous heights in the rain forests of the Olympic Peninsula.

What comes to mind when you think of Washington?

* The Space Needle, the recognized symbol of Seattle
* The Grand Coulee Dam, the largest concrete dam in the United States
* Mount St. Helens, an active volcano
* Yakama, Makah, Lummi, Quinault, and other Native American tribes carrying on their traditions
* Microsoft Corporation, one of the richest companies in the world and a leader in computer software
* Walla Walla's famous sweet onions
* Logging trucks carrying freshly cut trees to sawmills and pulp mills
* Orcas swimming off the coast of the San Juan Islands

Washington is a state filled with natural beauty and natural resources. It also has many successful businesses and a diverse population. Turn the page to discover the fascinating story of Washington.

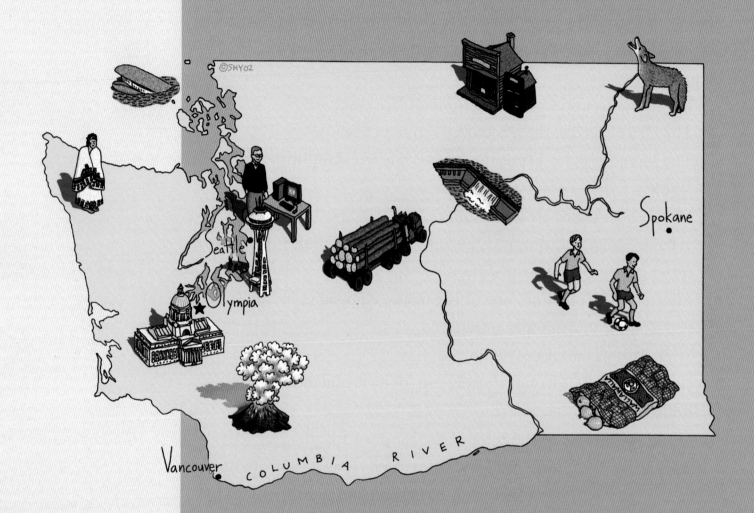

Spokane

Seattle

Olympia

Vancouver   COLUMBIA   RIVER

©SHY02

CHAPTER TWO

THE LAND OF WASHINGTON

Washington is in the northwest corner of the United States. This region is known as the Pacific Northwest. If you look on a map, this rectangular-shaped state looks as if it has a bite taken out of its northwest corner. Idaho borders Washington to the east. British Columbia, in Canada, lies to the north. Oregon is to the south, and the Pacific Ocean is to the west.

Washington is a big state. It covers 71,300 square miles (184,665 square kilometers), making it the nineteenth largest state in the country. Within this huge area, Washington has five land regions: the Coastal Range, the Puget Sound Lowlands, the Cascade Mountains, the Columbia Plateau, and the Rocky Mountains. Although the topography, or surface features, of each region varies greatly, all parts of Washington hold unique appeal.

A mother and daughter hike along the Pacific Crest Trail in the Cascade Mountains.

The Coastal Range covers a narrow strip of land in western Washington, along the Pacific Coast. In the northwestern corner of this region, a rugged slice of land juts into the Pacific Ocean. This is the Olympic Peninsula. Some of the wildest territory in North America is found there. Some parts haven't been explored yet. There are areas with dark forests, wild rivers, and rugged hills free of roads or trails.

Rising up from the peninsula are the Olympic Mountains. They reach an elevation (height) of 7,569 feet (2,309 meters) at Mount Olympus. Thick and jungle-like rain forests cover the western slopes of the mountains. Two such rain forests are the Quinquit Rain Forest and the Hoh Rain Forest. Parts of this region are showered with more than 100 inches (254 centimeters) of rain each year. These rich and moist forests can grow Douglas firs that are 300 feet (91 m) tall and 10 feet (3 m) wide. Logging and lumbering are the most important industries in the Coastal Range.

The temperate rain forest within Olympic National Park is home to many types of plants, including impressive trees covered with mosses.

PUGET SOUND LOWLANDS

East of the Coastal Range is the Puget Sound Lowlands. The lowlands border Puget Sound, a large, narrow saltwater inlet that begins with the Strait of Juan de Fuca. It continues into the heart of the western part of the state. Puget Sound has an irregular shoreline with big rocks or cliffs jutting into the water. It is dotted with about three hundred islands, which contribute to Washington's more than 3,000 miles (4,827 km) of shore-

Sea kayakers make their way down the Strait of Juan de Fuca.

line. Three in every four Washingtonians make their homes near Puget Sound. Poultry and dairy farms, as well as fruit orchards, thrive there.

THE CASCADE MOUNTAINS

East of the Puget Sound Lowlands are the Cascade Mountains. The Cascade Mountains extend north to south across central Washington, roughly dividing the state into east and west. Many of the rugged mountains found there were once active volcanoes. A volcano is a

CANADA

BRITISH
COLUMBIA

13,124 ft.	4,000 m
6,562 ft.	2,000 m
4,921 ft.	1,500 m
3,281 ft.	1,000 m
1,640 ft.	500 m
820 ft.	250 m
0	0

Strait of Georgia

San
Juan Is.

ROCKY
MTS.

Methow River

Okanogan River

Columbia River

Pend Oreille River

Franklin D.
Roosevelt
Lake

Strait of Juan de Fuca

Lake
Ozette

Lake
Crescent

OLYMPIC
MTS.

Lake
Quinault

Puget
Sound

Lake
Union

Lake Washington

Lake
Sammamish

Bellevue

Seattle

Cedar River

PUGET SOUND

Tacoma

LOWLANDS

Puyallup
River

⍟

Olympia

Mt. Rainier
14,410 ft./
4,392 m ▲

COASTAL
RANGE

Mt. St. Helens ▲

Lake
Chelan

Grand
Coulee
Dam

Moses
Lake

Spokane ●

COLUMBIA
PLATEAU

Columbia River

Snake River

IDAHO

C A S C A D E   M O U N T A I N S

PACIFIC
OCEAN

Vancouver

Columbia River

OREGON

N

0   25   50 mi.

0   25   50 km

mountain that serves as a vent or airway for the earth's crust. Occasionally, lava or steam bursts out from the top of the volcano.

Some of these volcanoes have erupted in recent times. Although Mount St. Helens had been dormant (inactive) for 123 years, it erupted on May 18, 1980. An earthquake triggered the top of the volcano to slide off and spew lava and ash all over. The eruption caused destruction for 100 miles (161 km), damaging plant and animal life. Ash flew to neighboring Idaho and Montana. Fifty-seven people in Washington were killed as a result of the eruption.

Several high peaks, such as Mount Rainier, are found in this region. Mount Rainier is the highest point in the state at 14,416 feet (4,397 m). It is actually a dormant volcano. After Mount Rainier, the four tallest mountains in Washington are Mount Baker, Mount Adams, Glacier Peak, and Mount St. Helens. Copper, gold, and coal are mined in this region, but mining is not a major industry.

Mount Rainier, referred to as "the Mountain" by locals, is a popular place for mountaineering (mountain climbing).

THE COLUMBIA PLATEAU

The Columbia Plateau covers much of the state east of the Cascade Mountains. A plateau is an elevated, level area of land. The Columbia Plateau was formed millions of years ago when a huge volcano erupted and covered the area with lava.

There are many differences within the plateau. The northwest corner has a broad rolling upland called the Waterville Plateau. In the northeast corner are rolling, wavelike hills made up of loess (pronounced *luhss*). Loess is fine, gray soil that has been blown into gentle hills by the wind. Called the Palouse Hills, this hilly country produces most of the state's wheat crop.

Between these two corners is a desert region. In some places, all the soil has been stripped away by erosion. The desolate rocky areas that remain are known as scablands, areas where patches of hard lava rock lie on the surface. Only plants that need little water, such as sagebrush, can grow there. This desert region is sparsely populated. Spokane is the largest city in the Columbia Plateau.

The gently rolling Palouse Hills attract many photographers as well as farmers.

Although the area gets little rainfall, the soil is very fertile. Farmers bring water from the Columbia River to the dry land by using pipes or ditches. This process is called irrigation. Irrigation makes it possible for farmers to raise their cattle and crops, allowing the region to prosper.

THE ROCKY MOUNTAINS

The Rocky Mountains are a major mountain system of western North America. The Rocky Mountains rise in the northeastern corner of Washington. These rugged mountains average from 3,000 to 7,000 feet (900 to 2,100 m) in elevation. They are mostly forested. From this region flows the Columbia River. It curves 1,240 miles (1,995 km) through central Washington to the Pacific Ocean. The Okanogan River is also located in this region, which is sometimes referred to as the Okanogan Highlands.

The major industry in this region is mining. Deposits of copper, gold, lead, magnesite, silver, and zinc are found there.

PLANTS AND WILDLIFE

More than half of Washington is covered with forests. Most of this plant life is found in western and northeastern Washington, an area that provides enough rainfall to support forest growth. Douglas fir, Sitka spruce, western hemlock, and ponderosa pines are a few of the

Ponderosa pines can be easily identified by their distinctive orange-brown bark.

trees found in the state. These specific trees are very valuable to the lumbering industry. The western hemlock is the state tree. Washington's small trees and shrubs include the dogwood and huckleberry. The state flower, the rhododendron, decorates the Evergreen State, along with trilliums, anemones, and Indian paintbrush.

All kinds of wildlife live in Washington. Mountain goats and cougars are found in the mountains. Bear, elk, and deer hide in the forests while grouse, eagles, heron, ducks, goldfinches, and geese fly above. Oysters, clams, and saltwater fish such as halibut and cod swim off the coast. Mammals such as whales, otters, and sea lions are also a common sight. Washington's rivers are home to freshwater fish such as rainbow trout, whitefish, and salmon. Some salmon can weigh up to 50 pounds (23 kilograms)!

RIVERS AND LAKES

All of Washington's rivers drain toward the Pacific Ocean. The most important river is the Columbia River. It is one of the nation's mightiest rivers. It enters Washington from Canada and flows south and west to form Washington's border with Oregon as it flows toward the Pacific Ocean. It covers more than 1,000 miles (1,609 km) in the state. Its tributaries, or waters that flow into and join the Columbia, include the Snake, Spokane, Okanogan, and Yakima rivers.

The Columbia River cuts through the Cascade Mountains to the Pacific Ocean.

Located on the Columbia River is Grand Coulee Dam, the largest concrete dam in the United States. There is enough concrete in the Grand Coulee Dam to build a highway that is 60 feet (18 m) wide, 3,000 miles (4,826 km) long, and 4 inches (10 cm) thick. The highway would stretch from Los Angeles to New York City!

Together, the Columbia River and the Grand Coulee Dam produce enormous amounts of hydroelectric power for Washingtonians. The force of the flowing water drives turbines (engines) that create electricity. The electricity is then used to run machines or to provide power to citizens. The power produced by the Columbia River is shared with other northwestern states.

FIND OUT MORE

Building the Grand Coulee Dam posed an interesting problem. When concrete is made, the chemicals that are mixed to make it give off heat. As concrete cools, it very slowly shrinks. What would have happened if this problem wasn't solved? What solution did the workers come up with?

Lake Chelan is a popular vacation destination in the Pacific Northwest.

The Snake River is the second largest river in the state. The Snake begins in Wyoming and winds its way north and west toward Washington. It is one of the most beautiful rivers in the country.

More than 8,000 lakes and ponds are scattered throughout Washington. Several lakes were created by glaciers, or thick sheets of ice. Glaciers found around Washington's mountains sometimes melt, sliding down and feeding lakes. The melted glaciers create pure, clean water. Washington's largest natural lake, Lake Chelan, was formed by glaciers. It is the third deepest freshwater lake in the nation and has some of the cleanest water in the United States. It extends nearly 400 feet (122 m) below sea level.

Numerous man-made lakes are found in Washington. These lakes, called reservoirs, were formed by dams for the purpose of collecting and storing water. The largest reservoir in Washington is the Franklin D. Roosevelt Lake, formed by the creation of the Grand Coulee Dam. The lake is used to store water for hydroelectric power and irrigation. Its total area is 125 square miles (323 sq km). Other major lakes in Washington include the Ozette, Crescent, and Quinault lakes. Lake Washington, Lake Sammamish, and Lake Union are important lakes west of the Cascades.

CLIMATE

The weather in Washington varies on either side of the Cascade Range. West of the range, winters are somewhat rainy and mild, and summers are cool. Seattle, a major city in this region, has an average temperature of 41° Fahrenheit (5° Celsius) in winter and 66° F (19° C) in summer.

The Olympic Peninsula gets about 135 inches (343 cm) of rain per year, contributing to the creation of one of the few rain forests in the United States. Snowfall is usually light along the coast, with only 5 inches (13 cm) per year. The coldest recorded winter temperature in Washington was near Mazama and Winthrop, where temperatures dipped to –48° F (–44° C) on December 30, 1968.

Eastern Washington has a dry climate. The Cascade Mountains cut off the moist winds blown in from the Pacific Ocean. Summers are hot and winters are cold. Spokane, a major city in the east, has an average temperature of 25° F (–4° C) in winter and 70° F (21° C) in summer.

EXTRA! EXTRA!

Washington holds the record for the heaviest winter snowfall in the United States. In 1970–1971, a blizzard buried Mount Rainier with 1,027 inches (2,609 cm) of snow. That's about eight stories high!

A cross-country skier makes her way through downtown Seattle after a snowstorm.

CHAPTER THREE

WASHINGTON THROUGH HISTORY

This drawing shows Main Street in Walla Walla during the 1890s.

About 11,000 years ago, a land bridge linked the northeastern part of Asia to North America. People traveled to North America by crossing this bridge. The very first people found huge animals, such as mastodons, woolly mammoths, and giant beavers roaming the land. People survived by hunting these prehistoric animals for food with sharp stone tools and weapons.

About 4,000 years ago, long before European explorers came, many Native Americans lived in what is now Washington. About seventy Native American tribes occupied the land. Some tribes lived on the Pacific coast and were known as coastal Native Americans. Others lived on the Columbia Plateau and were known as plateau or inland Native Americans. The coastal and inland tribes lived differently because they had different land resources and food sources.

The coastal Native Americans included major tribes such as the Chinook, Nooksak, Makah, and Puyallup. Life was good west of the Cascades along the Pacific Coast. The area had a fairly mild climate, and the land was rich with natural resources. Rivers were filled with fish. Forests were nurtured with rain and provided homes for deer and elk. The tribes had plenty of food available.

Native Americans made good use of the area's many cedar trees. The coastal tribes lived in permanent structures called longhouses. The longhouses were built near the ocean or along the Columbia River. They were made of cedar and were sometimes 100 feet (30 m) long and 40 feet (12 m) wide. A number of families could live together in one house. Cedar had a number of other uses as well. Native Americans used cedar trees to make clothing by pounding the bark until it became soft. Huge cedar logs were also carved into canoes, some of which were used to hunt whales in the ocean. To hunt, the natives used long wooden spears with sharp tips made from mussel shells. They also hunted large game in the forests, fished for salmon, and ate plants and roots.

The inland or plateau tribes lived east of the Cascades in the river valleys and plains. These included the Yakama, Cayuse, Nez

FIND OUT MORE

What customs did the tribes observe to prepare for whale hunting? How did they get the enormous whales onto shore?

Early Native Americans caught salmon in the Columbia River.

Perce, and Spokane tribes. These groups had to work much harder to survive. The climate was harsh and dry, and large game was scarce. Their villages were clustered along riverbanks so they could fish for salmon. The tribes honored the first salmon catch of the season with singing and dancing, after which the salmon was prepared and eaten. Then its bones were put back into the river in the hope that more salmon would come.

These Native Americans moved often to search for food. Their homes were made of movable wooden frames covered with mats of woven grass. In winter, they dug pits so they could live partially underground and have protection against the harsh cold and wind. Some homes were built next to cliffs to block the high winds.

They hunted deer, elk, moose, and other small animals and used the hides for clothing. They also gathered wild berries and edible roots. They ate fried cakes called pemmican made from dried meat, fish oil, and dried berries. This mixture would last through the winter without spoiling.

The coastal and inland tribes had little contact with one another. Sometimes they would meet on the Columbia River to trade. The plateau tribes traded skins, dried berries, mountain goat wool, and moccasins in exchange for cedar boxes, seashells, and dugout canoes from the coastal tribes. Often, dozens of tribal groups gathered at a fishing ground on the Oregon side of the river to trade, dance, or tell stories with Oregon nations. The coastal and plateau Native Americans lived peacefully until European settlers began to arrive.

In the late 1700s, Europeans began arriving in the Northwest. They came in search of the Northwest Passage, a waterway that linked the Atlantic and Pacific oceans. Over the course of more than 300 years, explorers discovered new lands and waterways while searching for this route.

In 1775, two Spaniards landed on Washington's coast. Bruno Heceta and Juan Francisco de la Bodega y Quadra of Spain claimed the Pacific Northwest for their country after sending an expedition there. To claim the land meant that this particular area of Washington belonged to Spain. A small settlement was built but it didn't last the year.

British sea captain James Cook explored the Pacific Coast in 1778. He was also looking for the Northwest Passage, and during his travels he charted (drew a map of) Washington's coast. When a crew member spotted a huge mountain, he said, "Surely it must be the home of the gods." He named the mountain Mount Olympus, after the Greek god Olympus.

Cook's crew reported an abundance of sea otter furs. These furs or pelts were popular in China, but sea otters were scarce there. As a result, many British merchants were attracted to the Pacific Coast because of the pelts, which could be sold in China for a huge profit.

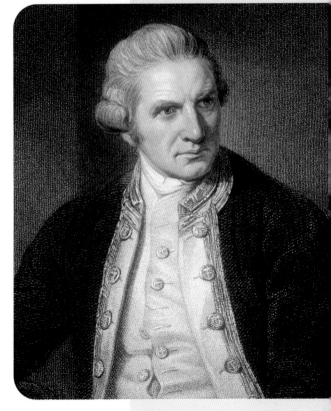

Captain James Cook was an explorer and mapmaker from Great Britain.

George Vancouver led an expedition of about 150 men to explore the Pacific Coast.

In 1792, England sent an expedition led by George Vancouver to check out the fur trading in the area. He stayed for two years exploring and mapping the coast. Vancouver named Puget Sound, along with Mount Rainier, Mount St. Helens, and Whidbey Island. This voyage strengthened Britain's claim to the area.

Robert Gray, an American sea captain and a fur trader from Boston, also led an expedition that year. He hoped to gather furs and trade them for tea from China. He risked sailing his boat, the *Columbia Rediviva*, through a treacherous passage from the Strait of Juan de Fuca. After fighting dangerous currents, he sailed into a broad river that was never before seen by Europeans. He named the river Columbia, after his ship. America now had its first claim to the region.

News of the Europeans' profitable fur trade in the Northwest spread throughout the United States. In 1803, United States president Thomas Jefferson sent explorers Meriwether Lewis and William Clark on an expedition. Jefferson hoped to find a water route from the Atlantic to the Pacific, open the land to Americans, and establish friendly relations with Native Americans.

With a party of soldiers and mountain men, Lewis and Clark trekked some 1,700 miles (2,736 km) over unknown and unexplored land between the Mississippi River and the Pacific Ocean. The eighteen-month journey was long and hard. Along the way, they met a Native American woman named Sacagawea (sometimes spelled Sacajawea), who accompanied the expedition as an interpreter. Together, they paddled up the Missouri River, crossed the Rocky Mountains by foot, and paddled down the Columbia River until they reached their destination, the Pacific Ocean. They blazed a new land route that opened the way for American settlers to travel to the Pacific Coast.

In the early 1800s, furs were still in high demand. The United States and Great Britain both claimed the Pacific Northwest. Each set up trading posts throughout the region, and the competition for land began.

John McLoughlin, a British Canadian, set up a trading post on the Columbia River in 1825. He was head of the British-owned Hudson's Bay Company. The post was called Fort Vancouver.

FAMOUS FIRSTS

- The Space Needle, built in 1961 in Seattle, has one of the world's first revolving restaurants.
- Seattle resident Edmund A. Smith invented the Iron Chink fish-cleaning machine in 1903. This machine was used in canneries to behead, de-fin, and gut fish.
- The first jet that took flight in the United States was built in Washington State in 1954.

Explorers Lewis and Clark reached the mouth of the Columbia River in 1805.

Mountain men braved cold, harsh winters to gather their furs.

Mountain men were among the first settlers to arrive. These men lived alone all winter, trapping animals in the mountains to collect their furs. It was a hard life. The mountain men had to survive harsh winters, grizzly bears, and Native American attacks. Those who survived would meet each year to trade their claims and collect payment.

Other settlers came to the region to teach the Christian religion to Native Americans. These people were called missionaries. In 1836, Americans Marcus and Narcissa Whitman settled with the Cayuse tribe in southeast Washington. Narcissa and another missionary, Eliza Spalding, were the first women to make the exhausting journey overland from New York to Oregon.

They traveled along the Oregon Trail, a route used by early pioneers. On descending a steep mountain, Narcissa Whitman described it as ". . . like winding stairs in its descent, and in some places almost perpendicular."

Along with the settlers came diseases, such as cholera, smallpox, and diphtheria.

EXTRA! EXTRA!

Timber, which was used for fuel, was often unavailable to early settlers traveling the Oregon Trail. Instead, pioneers used dried droppings, called buffalo chips, for fuel. The droppings acted as coals and produced a hot fire with no odors. The fire was then used to cook meals.

Native Americans never had contact with these diseases, so they had no protection against them. As a result, the diseases killed thousands.

Many Cayuse living near the Whitmans' mission also died of disease. The Cayuse didn't realize that the settlers were immune to these diseases. They became convinced that the missionaries were poisoning them so that Americans could claim the land. The Cayuse attacked the mission in 1847, killing the Whitmans and several other settlers. Despite this tragedy, settlers continued to come to the region.

Marcus Whitman preaches to members of his group at South Pass on the Oregon Trail.

EXTRA! EXTRA!

Although the United States and Britain had agreed to divide the land of Oregon, both countries claimed San Juan Island as their own. Crisis occurred in 1859, when an American farmer on the island, Lyman Cutlar, shot and killed a pig belonging to the Hudson's Bay Company. To prevent his arrest, American soldiers were sent to the island. The British followed suit. The dispute was not resolved until 1872, when San Juan Island was declared part of the United States. This incident became known as the Pig War.

THE OREGON TERRITORY

The United States and Britain agreed to divide the land as more people settled in the Northwest. The British moved their fur trading operations north to Canada. In 1848, the United States Congress created the Oregon Territory. The huge mass of land would later become the states of Washington, Oregon, Idaho, and parts of Montana and Wyoming.

The Oregon Territory was 1,500 miles (2,414 km) away from the nearest eastern town or western frontier. To reach this wilderness, people had to journey over the Oregon Trail from Missouri to Oregon. The trail was exhausting and dangerous, but thousands still came to settle the area for its rich farmland and new opportunities.

Between 1840 and 1860, about 300,000 settlers followed the Oregon Trail to California or the Oregon Territory. Families would form long wagon trains, one wagon after another. They challenged the rushing rivers, crossed twisted mountain passes, and lived in fear of Native American attacks. Diseases spread quickly from one wagon to another, killing thousands of people. Many people were buried along the Oregon Trail. Survivors who reached their destination built houses and farms in the Willamette Valley of Oregon.

About 13,000 settlers lived in the Oregon Territory by 1850. To encourage more people to settle there, Oregonians had passed the

Organic Act in 1843. This law gave as much as 640 acres (259 hectares) of land in Oregon Territory to any farm family willing to work the land for four years. It was one of the most generous land donations in American history.

Thousands of people were attracted by this gift. Settlements were set up in Tumwater in 1845, Olympia in 1846, Seattle in 1848, and Bellingham and Tacoma in 1852. Settlers in nearby California were hunting for gold, and rumors of their need for lumber and food spread to the Oregon Territory. Washington settlers began realizing the potential value of the Puget Sound country, where lumber and fishing were plentiful. The lumber was used to build houses and mining villages in California.

A wagon train makes its way through the Black Hills of South Dakota in 1887.

WHO'S WHO IN WASHINGTON?

Chief Seathl (1786–1866) was a chief of the Duwamish, Squamish, and other Native American groups of the Puget Sound area. He befriended the settlers and wanted a peaceful relationship with them. In 1855, he signed a treaty that established two reservations, or tracts of land, that the government agreed to set aside for their use. The city of Seattle is named for him.

WASHINGTON TERRITORY

In 1853, the Oregon territory was divided into Washington and Oregon. On March 2, President Millard Fillmore signed a law creating the Washington Territory. The territory, named for George Washington, the first president of the United States, included present-day Idaho and the western part of Wyoming. With only 3,965 settlers, Washington Territory could not apply to become its own state until its population reached 100,000. Isaac Stevens was appointed the first territorial governor. Olympia was its capital.

The new governor wanted Native Americans to give up their claim to land in Washington Territory to make room for more settlers. In 1855, 6,000 Native Americans in eastern Washington gathered with the governor to discuss a treaty, or formal agreement between the two groups. The governor was in a hurry to negotiate this treaty. He had heard stories of gold found in the area, and feared that Native Americans would learn of the land's possible value. He left the Native Americans with little choice. If they gave up their claim to the land, he promised to protect them on reservations, or land set aside just for them. They would be undisturbed by settlers and would receive food and clothing. If the Native Americans didn't choose to live on the reservations, there would be war. They'd risk losing their land altogether.

The Native Americans had trouble understanding the treaty, which was written in English. They also realized their bows and arrows were no match for the new settlers' guns. After three weeks, the Native Americans signed the treaty. Although Isaac Stevens had promised them two years to move, he began moving the villages right away to small reservations in places such as Colville.

The Native Americans were angry and fought back. However, they were so weakened from disease that they couldn't defend themselves. The tribes were sad, angry, and discouraged. This treaty and others like it fueled frustration and triggered wars that would rage through the territory from 1855 to 1858. Thousands of Native Americans died. Ultimately, they had no choice but to remain peacefully on their reservations.

While the tribes mourned their lost land, more settlers poured in from the east. The thick forests west of the Cascades provided many opportunities for lumberjacks (people who cut timber for sawmills). Washington had some of the world's largest trees. Sawmills, factories where wood was sawed and smoothed, cropped up around the region. Towns near the sawmills, especially around Puget Sound, grew into cities such as Tacoma. From these cities near the Pacific, lumber could be shipped all over the world.

Lumber fresh from sawmills was loaded onto ships in Puget Sound.

In the early 1850s, men greatly outnumbered women in the city of Seattle. The men needed brides, and children needed teachers. A man named Asa Mercer, president of the Territorial University in Seattle (now the University of Washington), invited women from the east to come west to be teachers. He promised many available men. Eleven women from Massachusetts agreed to come in 1864. They were referred to as the Mercer Girls. More women followed and they became teachers, wives, and grandmothers.

WASHINGTON BECOMES A STATE

In 1869 the final link in a transcontinental railroad was finished, connecting Nebraska and California. A local railroad line went through the town of Walla Walla. The Northern Pacific Railroad completed a second railroad line from the Great Lakes to Puget Sound in 1886, followed by the Great Northern rail line in 1893. Before the railroad, a trip to the eastern states took four long months by wagon. Travel and overland shipping of farm products and timber was now much easier.

Washington became less isolated after the railroad was built, making it easier for people to come and go from the territory.

The trains brought more settlers to the territory. Towns sprang up along the railroad routes. Many African-American, Chinese, and Japanese people came to work on the railroads. Between 1880 and 1890, the population increased from 75,000 to more than 350,000, enough people to apply for statehood. On November 11, 1889, Washington became the forty-second state. Elisha P. Ferry was elected Washington's first governor.

THE LAND OF PLENTY

Besides lumber, the valleys west of the Cascades offered rich farmland. However, life was not easy for the new settlers because almost everything had to be homemade. Items needed to survive, such as clothing, housing, tools, and food, were made with resources found on the land. Life in eastern Washington was even more difficult because of the cold winters and long distances between houses. Most people made a living by wheat farming and cattle and sheep ranching. The soil was fertile, but the land was dry. In 1890, ranchers began pumping water from nearby rivers to their fields. This process, called irrigation, allowed fruit to grow on dry grassland. Irrigation brought water to the land using ditches and pipes from rivers or lakes.

The first major irrigation project took place in Sunnyside on the Yakima River. With the new supply of water, farmers began to grow crops such as asparagus, tomatoes, and apples. Many people gave up ranching altogether to raise crops. Apple production boomed in the early 1900s, and more apples were grown in Washington than anywhere in the United States. Wheat also became an important crop in eastern Washington.

In 1896, gold was discovered in the Yukon and Alaska. Thousands of hopeful miners raced to Seattle to book a passage on board a ship heading north. Seattle became the main supply center for gold rushers. Merchants sold food, mining tools, and boat tickets. By 1900, Seattle's population doubled to more than 80,000 with the growth of gold rushing, lumbering, shipping, and fishing industries.

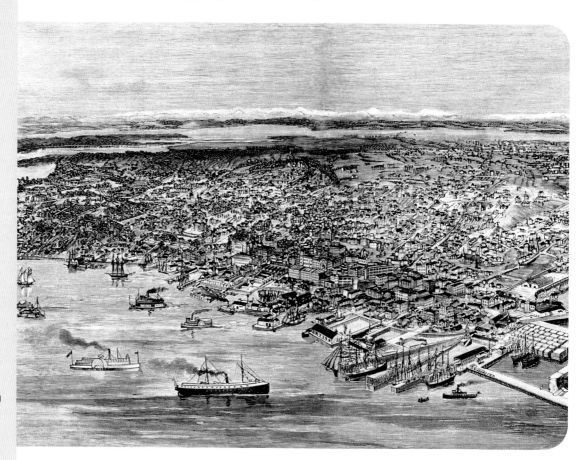

In the 1890s, Seattle was a growing, successful city in Washington State.

Spokane was Washington's fastest-growing city. Between 1889 and 1910, its population increased from 20,000 to 100,000. It became Washington's second largest city because of railroad construction, electricity, and the opportunity for merchants to provide services to miners in nearby Idaho.

WHAT'S IN A NAME?

The names of many places in Washington have interesting origins.

Name	Comes From or Means
Bremerton	Named for German immigrant William Bremmer
Walla Walla	Native American word meaning "place of many waters"
Spokane	From the Native American word *spehkunne*, meaning "children of the sun" or "sun people"
Lake Chelan	Native American word meaning "deep water"
Mount Rainier	Explorer George Vancouver named the mountain in honor of Rear-Admiral Peter Rainier of the Royal Navy
Omak	Native American word *omache* meaning "good medicine" or "plenty"

WORLD WAR I AND THE GREAT DEPRESSION

The biggest war that the world had ever seen started in 1914. It was called World War I (1914–1918). Many European countries and other nations were involved, and by 1917, the United States had also joined the war. Although it was mostly fought in Europe, Washington contributed to the war effort at home. Washington farmers grew crops and factories produced canned foods to help feed the soldiers. Shipyards in Tacoma and Seattle built warships, and the Fort Lewis army base was built near Tacoma. Washington's economy enjoyed the sudden boom.

By the 1930s, the Great Depression brought the economy to a halt. Starting in 1929, the depression was a time of low business activity when few people earned money. People who had invested in stocks lost all their money when the stock market crashed. One in three people lost their jobs. Banks closed, people lost their homes, businesses failed, and farmers abandoned their farms. More than three-quarters of the sawmills in Washington closed. Hundreds of thousands of people were nearly starving.

Across the country, government programs were started in an effort to create jobs. These programs employed people to build public works projects, such as roads, parks, and schools. In 1933, the United States government began a dam-building program in Washington. Thousands of Washingtonians were employed to build the dams, two of which were built on the Columbia River. The Bonneville Dam was completed in 1937, and the Grand Coulee Dam was finished in 1942. The Grand Coulee Dam is the largest concrete structure in the United States.

During the depression, thousands of workers came to Washington to help build the Grand Coulee Dam.

Washington began to recover from the depression when World War II (1939–1945) started in Europe. The United States entered the war in 1941, after Japanese planes bombed a United States naval base in Pearl Harbor, Hawaii, and killed more than 2,000 people. Thousands of Washingtonians joined the United States Armed Forces to help fight the war.

Washington also contributed in other ways. The state's many ports were good places to build warships and aircraft. Thousands of people came to work in the shipyards. Factories used hydroelectric power to produce aluminum and aluminum products. Because of its access to cheap electricity, Washington began to produce more aluminum than any other state. Factories began making airplanes out of aluminum. The Boeing Airplane Company developed and produced B-17 and B-29 bombers. Boeing employed almost 45,000 people.

In the city of Hanford, plutonium was produced to make atomic bombs. An atomic bomb is a weapon that releases atomic energy when it explodes. They are the most powerful weapons in existence. Atomic bombs can cause destruction and death for miles. Two of these bombs were dropped on Japan to end World War II in 1945.

During the war, Boeing's aircraft, especially the B-17, became legendary for their strength and durability.

The war brought jobs and money to Washington. It also brought an opportunity for prejudice. Prejudice is when someone judges another person, usually because of race or color. Because the United States was fighting against Japan, many people of Japanese ancestry living in the United States were accused of being spies during the war.

The United States government forced many Japanese Americans into prison camps that were surrounded by barbed wire and guarded by soldiers. Thousands of Japanese Americans were taken to an assembly center in Puyallup and then to camps in California and Idaho. When they returned home after the war, many found their possessions gone, their fields overgrown, and their savings taken away.

Japanese Americans were ordered out of their homes and into prison camps during World War II.

When the war ended, Washington prospered once again. Houses and shopping centers were built on land that was once farmed. The Puget Sound region saw enormous population growth as soldiers came to live in Washington and others returned home.

In April 1962, Seattle hosted the World's Fair, Century 21, to promote tourism. The World's Fair was a six-month international fair consisting of many agriculture, science, and craft exhibits. The Space Needle was built as the central attraction. Nearly ten million people visited the World's Fair that year.

Many visitors to the World's Fair got their first glimpse of Seattle and the Pacific Northwest in 1962.

In the 1960s, Washingtonians realized that their rivers and lakes were being polluted. Factories disposed of their wastes improperly, and chemicals leaked into the rivers. Also, forests were being cut down faster than they could grow. Washington decided to take action. The state started cleaning up its waterways, and oil tankers were no longer allowed in Puget Sound. Citizens began recycling. Logging was limited in order to preserve wildlife.

Life was peaceful for Washingtonians until March 1980, when Mount St. Helens began to rumble and give off steam. On May 18, the

In the area surrounding Mount St. Helens, many living things died as a result of the ash emitted from the eruption.

9,677-foot (2,950-m) volcano erupted. Earthquakes rattled the region, and debris was thrown 12 miles (19 km) into the sky. Eastern Washington was covered in a cloud of ash so thick it turned day into night. The ash settled everywhere, including nearby towns and other parts of eastern Washington, Idaho, and Montana. Fifty-seven people near the volcano were killed, along with thousands of animals, birds, and fish. Over 1,400 feet (427m) of the mountain was blasted off.

Today, Washington faces different issues. Traffic has become a problem thanks to a huge increase in the state's population. Many people use vehicles for transportation to and from work. Thousands of people traveling to cities near Puget Sound create traffic jams. If more people come to the Seattle area, it will get worse.

Washingtonians have long realized that preserving nature is also vital. Salmon have become endangered in Washington for many reasons, including overfishing. Many people feel that dams should be removed so that salmon can reach their spawning destination (the place where they reproduce). However, this would cost the state money. To make things worse, the population of sea lions has greatly increased on the West Coast in recent years. Sea lions are predators of salmon, and many people worry about the effect these animals have on the salmon population. Studies are now being done to determine how to best protect these fish. In the meantime, schools are teaching children how to help save the salmon, and the government has formed groups to promote protection.

With the growth of new industries such as computer software companies, Washington promises a growing economy in the twenty-first century. Today's Washingtonians are more educated than ever before. The future of Washington looks bright, and its people welcome new challenges.

In 2005, Seattle drivers spent an average of 45 hours stuck in traffic. That was an improvement—in 1995, the average was 52 hours!

CHAPTER FOUR

GOVERNING WASHINGTON

The design of the capitol is similar to that of the Acropolis, an important site in Athens, Greece.

When Washington became a state in 1889, the state constitution was written and adopted. Washington is still governed by this original constitution, which is a set of rules and principles by which the state is run. The constitution also explains what rights are guaranteed to the people of Washington.

Washington's constitution has changed slightly over the years. Changes, called amendments, may be made by the legislature. The legislature is a group of people who make laws for the state. If more than half of voters agree to the change, then the amendment becomes law. Washington's constitution has been amended eighty-three times since 1889. The most recent amendment was made in 1988.

The constitution divides Washington's government into three branches: the executive, legislative, and judicial. These three branches work together to make sure the state runs smoothly.

EXECUTIVE BRANCH

The executive branch is responsible for making sure that laws in Washington are enforced. The governor is head of the executive branch. The people elect the governor to a four-year term. There is no limit to the number of terms that he or she can serve. The governor signs and approves bills (proposed laws), and communicates with other state governments. He or she can also call the state militia to action in times of emergency.

Other members of the executive branch include the lieutenant governor, secretary of state, treasurer, attorney general, state auditor, superintendent of public instruction, insurance commissioner, and commissioner of public lands. Each member is elected to a four-year term.

Members of the executive branch have many responsibilities. The lieutenant governor acts as governor when the present governor cannot. The secretary of state is responsible for supervising state elections and collecting and preserving historical information about the state. The state treasurer is the main financial officer. He or she keeps track of the state's money.

The attorney general is the state's lawyer. His or her responsibilities include giving legal advice to the governor and state officials. The state auditor's job is to account for money the government spends. The superintendent of public instruction is responsible for Washington's education program. The insurance commissioner helps protect people who buy insurance in the state. Lastly, the commissioner of public lands is responsible for protecting Washington's natural resources. He or she manages or conserves Washington's forests and agricultural lands.

Senators meet in the senate chamber to discuss new laws.

LEGISLATIVE BRANCH

The legislative branch is responsible for making the laws of the state. This branch consists of two groups: a 49-member senate and a 98-member house of representatives. Together they are known as the legislature and its members are called legislators. Senators are elected to four-year terms. Members of the house are elected to two-year terms.

Bills, or proposed laws, are created by the legislature and sent to the governor for approval. Once the governor signs a bill, it becomes law. If the governor refuses to sign the bill, the legislature can vote to overturn the governor's decision if the majority of both houses agree. This allows the legislature to pass a bill even without the governor's approval.

JUDICIAL BRANCH

The judicial branch interprets, or explains, the laws and decides if someone has broken the law. Courts and judges make up the judicial branch. Many cases begin in district and municipal courts. These courts handle cases involving divorce, juveniles (young offenders), and minor civil and criminal cases such as assault, littering, and traffic tickets. Judges for these courts are elected to four-year terms.

The next court is the superior court. This court handles more serious cases and uses a jury. A jury is a group of citizens who decide whether a person is guilty or innocent by listening to facts and evidence.

The court of appeals hears cases that have already been heard by a lower court (district, municipal, or superior court). If a person feels that his or her case was unfairly judged in any of these courts, he or she may request a new trial, called an *appeal*, by the court of appeals. The court of appeals has twenty judges. Each is elected to a six-year term.

The most powerful court in the state is the state supreme court. This court hears appeals from lower courts. The supreme court's decision is final. Nine justices (judges) serve six-year terms on the supreme court.

Elementary schoolchildren descend the steps of the Temple of Justice, home of the Washington State supreme court.

TAKE A TOUR OF OLYMPIA, THE STATE CAPITAL

Set on the shores of the southernmost point of Puget Sound is Olympia, Washington's state capital. Olympia is named after the Olympic Mountains, which can be seen from the city.

According to the 2000 census, Olympia has a population of 42,514. Although government is the city's main business, many other important

WASHINGTON GOVERNORS

Name	Term	Name	Term
Elisha P. Ferry	1889–1893	Arthur B. Langlie	1941–1945
John Harte McGraw	1893–1897	Monrad C. Wallgren	1945–1949
John Rankin Rogers	1897–1901	Arthur B. Langlie	1949–1957
Henry McBride	1901–1905	Albert D. Rosellini	1957–1965
Albert Edward Mead	1905–1909	Daniel J. Evans	1965–1977
Samuel G. Cosgrove	1909	Dixy Lee Ray	1977–1981
Marion E. Hay	1909–1913	John Spellman	1981–1985
Ernest Lister	1913–1919	Booth Gardner	1985–1993
Louis Folwell Hart	1919–1925	Mike Lowry	1993–1997
Roland H. Hartley	1925–1933	Gary Locke	1997–2005
Clarence D. Martin	1933–1941	Christine Gregoire	2005–

WASHINGTON STATE GOVERNMENT

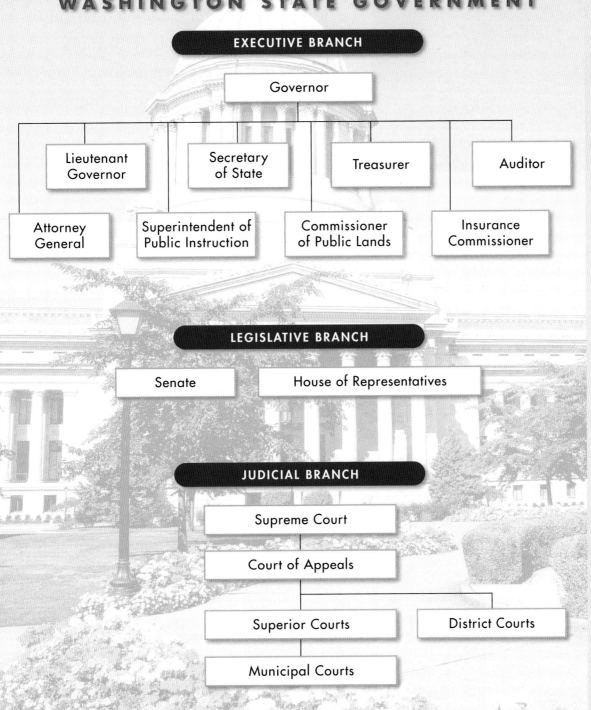

EXECUTIVE BRANCH

Governor

Lieutenant Governor

Secretary of State

Treasurer

Auditor

Attorney General

Superintendent of Public Instruction

Commissioner of Public Lands

Insurance Commissioner

LEGISLATIVE BRANCH

Senate

House of Representatives

JUDICIAL BRANCH

Supreme Court

Court of Appeals

Superior Courts

District Courts

Municipal Courts

A chandelier weighing 5 tons hangs from the inside of the capitol dome.

FIND OUT MORE

Washington's capitol building resembles one other capitol in the United States. Can you name which one?

industries are located there. Tourism; manufacturing; lumber mills; fishing; and shipping also employ the people of Olympia.

On a high bluff overlooking Puget Sound stands the state capitol, completed in 1928. Forty-two granite steps lead up to its entrance. These steps symbolize Washington's place as the forty-second state in the Union. Details were delicately carved into the building by a team of thirty artists who carved into the sandstone, marble, and wood for five years. The capitol stands twenty-eight stories high.

Inside you can catch glimpses of state senators and representatives in action. You can also walk around the campus to the State Capitol Museum or the Executive Mansion. The State Capitol Museum has exhibits detailing Washington's rich history during territorial and early statehood days. The museum displays natural history and science exhibits, local art, and rare Native American cedar-bark baskets. You can even see inside a Native American house and handle traditional tools.

Since 1909, every governor has lived in the Executive Mansion. This twenty-six-room house was built in 1908. The mansion was built quickly because it was meant to be a temporary place for state officials to entertain visitors from other countries or states. It is the oldest building on the Capitol Campus. Inside, tourists can see antique furnishings that are two hundred years old.

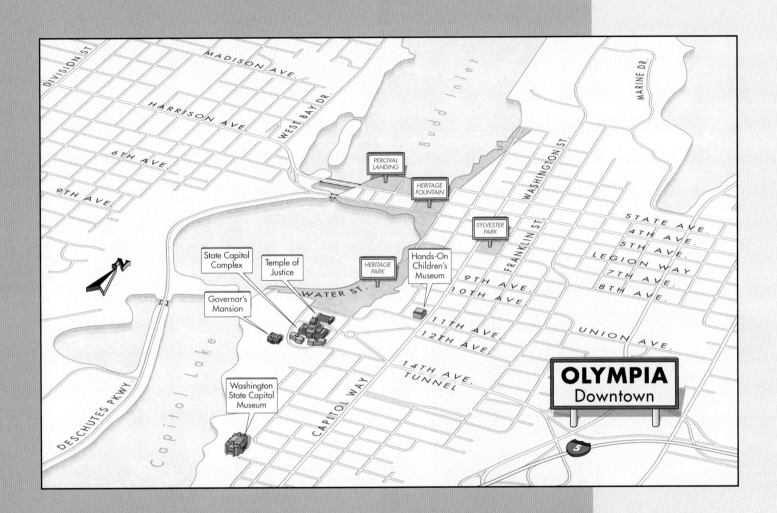

MADISON AVE.

DIVISION ST.

HARRISON AVE.

WEST BAY DR.

6TH AVE.

9TH AVE.

Budd Inlet

MARINE DR.

WASHINGTON ST.

PERCIVAL LANDING

HERITAGE FOUNTAIN

STATE AVE.
4TH AVE.
5TH AVE.
LEGION WAY
7TH AVE.
8TH AVE.

SYLVESTER PARK

FRANKLIN ST.

State Capitol Complex

Temple of Justice

HERITAGE PARK

Hands-On Children's Museum

9TH AVE.
10TH AVE.

Governor's Mansion

WATER ST.

11TH AVE.

12TH AVE.

UNION AVE.

Capitol Lake

DESCHUTES PKWY.

14TH AVE. TUNNEL

CAPITOL WAY

OLYMPIA
Downtown

Washington State Capitol Museum

5

If you happen to be in Olympia in the fall, stop by the Capitol Lake Fish Ladder to see thousands of Chinook salmon swim from the Pacific Ocean to the Deschutes River. Where large dams block a river, fish ladders provide a way for salmon to get around the dam. The "ladder" is a group of pools, with each pool a bit higher than the other. The salmon swim up the ladder by leaping from one pool to the next. The problem with the ladder is that many fish are unable to make the journey up the ladder and small salmon die along the way.

One of Olympia's historic sites includes a large boulder in Sylvester Park. This boulder marks the end of the Oregon Trail. This trail was used by thousands of pioneers hoping to reach the Pacific Northwest in the early 1800s. For a mix of history and scenic beauty, visit the Historic Westside Grocery. You can stand on the porch of this 1904 corner store and get a good view of Olympia and Mount Rainier in the distance.

Finally, the Temple of Justice is an interesting place to visit. This 1920 structure houses the state supreme court and the law library. It is open for tours on weekdays.

Salmon pass through the fish ladder at Bonneville Dam.

CHAPTER FIVE

THE PEOPLE AND PLACES OF WASHINGTON

Washington is one of the nation's fastest-growing states. According to the 2000 census, 5,894,121 people live in the Evergreen State. Since 1990, the population has increased by almost 900,000 people. New computer software and technology businesses have attracted many people to Washington.

The state has an average population density of 86 people per square mile (33 per sq km), although the population is unevenly distributed. Very few people live in parts of eastern Washington, while some parts of western Washington are crowded. Most people prefer to live near the ocean because of the mild climate. More than 8 in 10 Washingtonians live in cities or towns, especially near the Puget Sound area. Seattle is the state's largest city, with a population of 563,374. Other large cities include Tacoma, Bellevue, Everett, Spokane, and Walla Walla.

Fish vendors show off their wares at Pike Place Market, a public market in Seattle.

Children take part in the annual Pow Wow Day at Harrah Elementary School on the Yakama Indian reservation.

Nine in ten Washingtonians were born in the United States. Many can trace their roots back to parts of Europe, Asia, and Scandinavia. People of European descent have ancestors from Germany, Poland, Hungary, Russia, Italy, and Spain.

In 2000, fewer than 1 in 10 Washingtonians was African-American. One in 10 Washingtonians belongs to other ethnic groups such as Native American, Asian American, and Hispanic American.

At one time, Native Americans were the only people living on the land we now call Washington. Today, about 107,219 Native Americans live there. This is a small number compared to Washington's total population, but compared to other states it is large. In fact, Washington has the sixth largest Native American population in the United States, with twenty-eight federally recognized tribes.

One in four Native Americans in Washington lives on one of the state's twenty-seven reservations. The largest reservation belongs to the

Yakama. It is located in southwestern Washington and contains 1,130,000 acres (457,311 ha) of land.

Other reservations in Washington include the Colville Reservation and the Spokane Reservation in northeastern Washington; and the Hoh and Quinault reservations on the Washington coast.

WORKING IN WASHINGTON

Today, manufacturing is the leading industry in Washington. One in every six people works in a factory that manufactures products. Thousands work in factories that produce airplanes, ships, missiles, spacecraft, and transportation equipment. The leading industrial areas are Seattle and Tacoma around Puget Sound. Because Washington is closer to Asia and other eastern countries than most other states, many of Washington's products are shipped across the ocean to Japan, China, Korea, Mexico, and Canada.

The second most important type of manufacturing in Washington is food processing (preparing foods for sale in stores). Fish, berries, vegetables, and fruit are

Cargo ships are a familiar sight on the Pacific coast. The state's major seaports include Seattle, Tacoma, Longview, and Kalama.

51

Pulp mills in Washington run around the clock and employ thousands of workers.

cleaned and packaged, canned, or frozen. Some of Washington's huge apple crops are made into candy, vinegar, or applesauce.

Washington also makes more computer software than most other states. Microsoft is one of the most successful and well-known computer software companies in the world. It is located northeast of Seattle in the city of Redmond.

Another major industry in Washington is forestry. Washington is one of the leading producers of lumber, wood pulp, and paper products. In fact, Washington is ranked second among other states in lumber producing. The most profitable wood is softwood such as the Douglas fir and western hemlock. Nearly half of the wood is used for lumber, and the rest is used for pulp or plywood.

Jobs that provide a service to others employ more Washingtonians than any other type of work. The service industry includes restaurants, health care, stores, education, and tourism, among other things. Tourism, the business of providing information, accommodations, transportation, and other services to visitors, is the fastest-growing part of the economy. Washington's beautiful scenery and awesome attractions such as the Grand Coulee Dam and Mount St. Helens bring millions of tourists to the state each year. Other forms of tourism include whale watching, mountain climbing, and cruising to Alaska from Washington ports.

Almost half of Washington's total land area is devoted to farmland. There are approximately 34,000 farms in Washington. Most farms are located in the irrigated areas around the Columbia and Snake rivers, the Puget Sound region, and in eastern Washington. The irrigated areas generally grow grapes, potatoes, cherries, and apples, along with some livestock. The Puget Sound region has many greenhouses and nurseries that produce flowers and flower bulbs. The leading field crop is wheat, grown mostly in eastern Washington. Other important farm products include poultry, eggs, dairy products, berries, tulip bulbs, and pears. Washington leads the nation in apple production.

WHO'S WHO IN WASHINGTON?

Bill Gates (1955–) started writing computer programs at age fourteen. In 1975, he started Microsoft Corporation, a company that makes software for computers. Today his company is a worldwide leader in computer software, making Gates one of the richest men in the world. Gates grew up in Seattle.

Washington apples are sold in all fifty states.

Washingtonians love their apples. Follow this simple recipe for a way to eat and play with your food! Be sure to ask an adult for help.

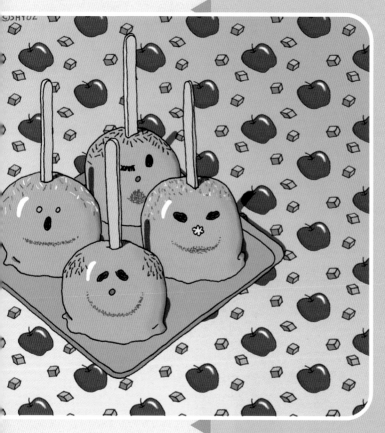

FUNNY FACE CARAMEL APPLES

4 popsicle sticks
4 medium apples
1 14-oz. package of caramels
2 tablespoons water
Raisins, sprinkles, or candies

1. Insert popsicle sticks into bottoms of apples.
2. Place unwrapped caramels and water in a 1-quart pan.
3. Cook, stirring constantly, over low heat until melted.
4. Dip apples into caramels, using a spoon to help cover them completely.
5. Place covered apples on a plate lined with wax paper or parchment paper.
6. Use raisins, sprinkles, or candies to make funny faces on the apples.
7. Freeze for 15 minutes and enjoy!

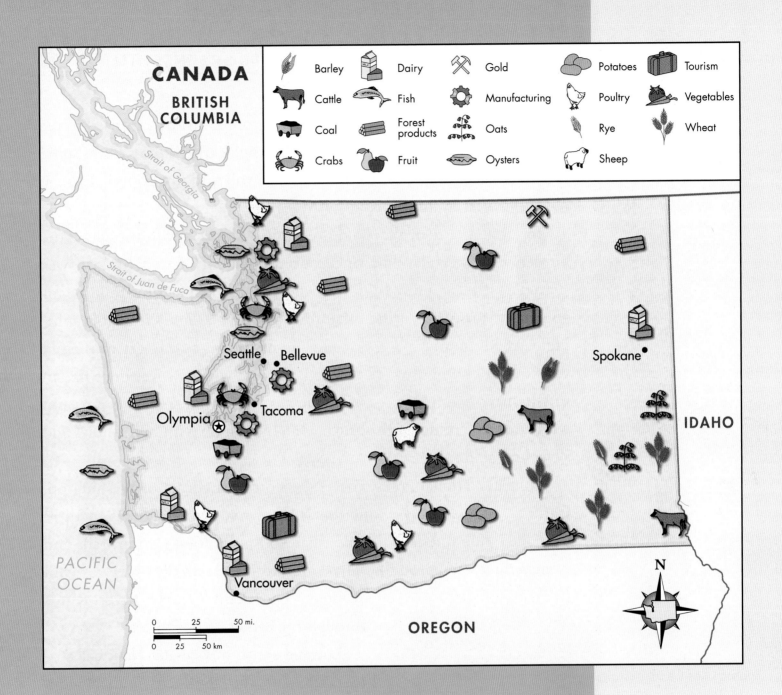

CANADA

BRITISH COLUMBIA

	Barley		Dairy		Gold		Potatoes		Tourism
	Cattle		Fish		Manufacturing		Poultry		Vegetables
	Coal		Forest products		Oats		Rye		Wheat
	Crabs		Fruit		Oysters		Sheep		

Strait of Georgia

Strait of Juan de Fuca

PACIFIC OCEAN

Seattle
Bellevue
Spokane

Olympia
Tacoma

IDAHO

Vancouver

OREGON

N

0 25 50 mi.

0 25 50 km

TAKE A TOUR OF THE EVERGREEN STATE

Eastern Washington

Welcome to rugged northeastern Washington. Don't be surprised to see tumbleweeds, canyons, coyotes, or free-range cattle as you travel some of the lonesome highways in this area. You will find towns similar to the old Wild West in this dry and warm region.

To catch a taste of the Wild West, visit a ghost town just below the border with Canada. The once booming town of Old Molson was started in 1900 as a mining town, where many people came to mine for gold. After many years, and other towns hinting at interest in gold mining, Old Molson was abandoned. The memories still linger in the old weathered buildings, where you can imagine what life was once like in this pioneer community. The town has been preserved as a museum with many interesting sights, such as an old saloon with bullet holes and silver and gold mines.

Colville National Forest covers the northeast corner of Washington. Caribou, moose, wolves, and black bears make their homes in these unspoiled pine forests. The forest has 400 miles (644 km) of trails and twenty-three campgrounds. There are fifty-five lakes on which to swim or boat. The Pend Oreille River winds through the center of this forest.

Located south of Colville National Forest is Spokane, the largest city in the region. It is home to 195,629 Washingtonians. The centerpiece of downtown Spokane is Spokane Falls, a waterfall on the Spokane

EXTRA! EXTRA!

Spokane was the smallest city ever to host the World's Fair, Expo 1974. The fair was open for six months, and five million people visited. That is roughly twenty-eight times Spokane's population!

Spokane is the largest city between Seattle and Minneapolis.

River. In the late 1800s, the falls were used to power the first flour and sawmills of the growing city. Today, residents appreciate the beauty of the falls and take time to enjoy the view from the riverbanks and pedestrian bridges.

West of Spokane is the Grand Coulee Dam. This 46-story concrete dam is the nation's largest dam. Visitors can ride up in a glass elevator to see a fantastic view of the spillway where the water pours out. At night, the largest laser show in the world takes place there, with beautiful lights that dance across the face of the dam.

Southeast of the dam is the city of Pullman, home of Washington State University's main campus. The university has several

Visitors get a view of Grand Coulee Dam from the top.

branches throughout the state, including Spokane and Vancouver. This higher education center offers students the opportunity to become veterinarians, pharmacists, engineers, architects, nurses, and more.

Next, head southwest to Walla Walla, a city famous for its sweet onions. Onions grown there are mild enough to be eaten like apples. You can visit the Fort Walla Walla Museum Complex, and tour fourteen pioneer buildings that have been restored to their original condition. There you'll find out how fur traders and pioneers lived during the 1800s.

The Tri-Cities—Kennewick, Richland, and Pasco—are also located in southeastern Washington. These large cities are connected by the Columbia, Snake, and Yakima rivers. At Kennewick you can visit the Columbia Park Family Fishing Pond. At this first-of-its-kind fishery project, children can fish the waters of a pond stocked with catfish or play at a large community park playground. It features slides, a pirate ship, towers, turrets, and a musical play station. In Richland, the Columbia River Exhibition of History, Science, and Technology features hands-on exhibits and activities about the Columbia Basin region. Visitors can learn about hydroelectric power and explore the history of the Columbia River.

The Inter City Bridge crosses the Columbia River in the Tri-Cities area of eastern Washington.

CANADA

BRITISH
COLUMBIA

Legend:
- National park, forest, or recreation area
- Highway
- ⍟ Capital city
- ● City
- ▲ State park
- ■ Tourist site

Molson

COLVILLE
NATIONAL FOREST

Bellingham

San Juan Is.

Makah
Cultural &
Research
Center

Strait of Georgia

Strait of Juan de Fuca

Winthrop   Omak   Kettle Falls

Okanogan

LAKE CHELAN NAT'L
RECREATION AREA

Grand Coulee
Dam

Everett

Puget Sound

OLYMPIC
NATIONAL
PARK

Edmonds

Kirkland
Bellevue

Leavenworth
Bavarian Village

Spokane

Seattle

Bremerton   Kent   Renton

Federal Way

Covington

Tacoma

Olympia

MOUNT
RAINIER
NATIONAL
PARK

Ellensburg

90

90

IDAHO

Pullman

PACIFIC
OCEAN

Pasco

Yakama Nation
Cultural Center

82   Richland

Sacajawea
State Park

Kelso

Kennewick   Walla Walla

Vancouver

Columbia
Gorge

0   25   50 mi.

0   25   50 km

OREGON

N

At Pasco, children can play laser tag at the Playground of Dreams in Columbia Park or relax at Sacajawea State Park. Sacajawea State Park was named in honor of the young Native American woman who accompanied Lewis and Clark on their expedition to the Pacific Northwest. At the park, visitors can picnic, fish, boat, or waterski.

Central Washington

Step back to the 1800s in the town of Winthrop, located in north central Washington. This town has preserved history well and gives visitors a glimpse into yesteryear. You can enjoy strolling on the old wooden boardwalks or watch a cattle drive. You may have to pinch yourself to remember what year it really is!

Winthrop is also known for its cross-country skiing. There are more than 100 miles of cross-country trails in the area. Culture lovers should be sure to attend Methow Valley Chamber Music Festival, held every summer.

Not far from Winthrop is Omak, one of the largest towns in central Washington. Omak is known for its annual stampedes. In a stampede, professional rodeo riders dash their horses down steep hills that seem like cliffs. Animal rights activists (people who promote the safety and well-being of animals) protest this event every year because many horses have died in this stampede. Other events include a powwow (a Native American meeting and dance describing a tribe's culture and history), a Native-American drum competition, and a demolition derby.

(opposite)
A windsurfer jumps the waves at the Columbia Gorge near Bingen.

60

Nearby at Lake Chelan National Recreation Area you can go horseback riding, camping, or hiking. Visitors can also swim the clean and fresh waters of Lake Chelan, the third deepest lake in the nation. It is 1,486 feet (453 m) deep.

If you like action and adventure, visit the Columbia Gorge. A gorge is a deep, narrow valley that is usually steep and rocky. The Columbia Gorge forms a massive wind funnel when warm desert air hits cool coastal breezes. The winds affect the water, and the result is wild waters perfect for wind surfing, kayaking, or white-water rafting. On a bluff overlooking the Columbia Gorge is the Gorge Amphitheater. People can hike along scenic trails to this natural outdoor theater with the top open to the sky. At the Gorge Amphitheater, famous entertainers perform throughout the summer.

The Yakama Nation Museum and Cultural Heritage Center includes a museum, theater, restaurant, and gift shop.

After leaving the gorge, head north to Toppenish, where you can learn about Washington's earliest residents at the Yakama Nation Museum and Cultural Heritage Center. The center was created to preserve the Yakama culture and to teach the public about their nation. It consists of a museum with a 76-foot- (23-m-) high winter lodge. The Yakama built large lodges in winter where several families could live together.

You can learn about a different culture in Leavenworth, a town at the foot of the Cascade Mountains that is modeled after a Bavarian village. Bavaria is part of Germany, a European country from which many immigrants came in the late 1800s. This authentic German village is famous for its delicious German food, including sauerkraut, sausages, and schnitzel. Dancing, theater, and festivals year-round celebrate the Bavarian culture.

In the 1960s, many of the buildings in Leavenworth were remodeled to adopt a Bavarian theme.

The state's most popular tourist attraction is Mount Rainier National Park on mighty Mount Rainier. This dormant volcano is covered by more than 35 square miles (91 sq km) of snow and ice year-round. The park includes outstanding examples of old-growth forests and glacier-fed rivers. Visitors can hike, snowshoe, or ski on the 300 miles (483 km) of park trails.

Along the Coast and Puget Sound

Many of Washington's major cities lie in the Puget Sound area. One of these cities is Everett, home to about 91,488 people. This city served as the headquarters of the Boeing Company for more than eighty years. Boeing's manufacturing complex in Everett was recognized by the *Guinness Book of World Records* as the largest building in the world by volume. It covers 98.3 acres (40 ha) and is so large that is requires its own fire department, security force, and medical clinic! Visitors can tour the factory to see how the latest aircraft are built.

Seattle, Washington's largest city, is often thought of as a rainy city. In fact, Seattle only receives about 34 inches (86 cm) of rain each year. Whether rain or shine, Seattle has many things to see and do. Start your tour of Seattle by taking the monorail to the Seattle Center. The Seattle Center is a 74-acre (30-ha) development that was built for the World's Fair in 1962. The center offers a roller coaster, a Ferris wheel, and arcades.

Another Seattle attraction that was built for the fair is the Space Needle. It resembles a flying saucer on a tripod, rising 605 feet (184 m) into

From the observation deck of the Space Needle, visitors can get a good view of Seattle, as well as Mount Rainier and Puget Sound.

the air. Visitors can ride up inside the needle to get a panoramic view of the city from the observation deck.

At Seattle's Woodland Park Zoo you can see wild animals such as bears, giraffes, monkeys, African lions, and hippos roaming freely in natural settings. It is also home to the famous baby elephant, Hansa.

The Seattle Aquarium offers children a chance to learn about marine and freshwater life in the Northwest. There is a spectacular underwater viewing dome that offers visitors a view of a 400,000-gallon (1,510,000-liter) fish tank filled with fish. Large sharks circle the tank looking for fish to prey on. Each day there is a public feeding, and lights are turned on at night to get a better view of salmon, cod, or rockfish.

If you love music, Seattle is the place to be. The Experience Music Project is a one-of-a-kind music museum. You can learn about music through interactive exhibits that let you play an instrument or create your own music. You can see the memorabilia of famous musicians, including guitars that belonged to stars such as Jimi Hendrix and Bob Dylan. Learning about music has never been so much fun.

WHO'S WHO IN WASHINGTON?

Jimi Hendrix (1942–1970) is considered by some to be the greatest electric guitarist of all time. He had a short career with a rock group called the Jimi Hendrix Experience. Hendrix was born in Seattle.

The Seattle Mariners take time out for the national anthem at Safeco Field.

For devoted sports fans, Seattle boasts its own football, baseball, and basketball teams. You can watch the Seattle Seahawks play football at Qwest Field. The Seattle Mariners play baseball at their stadium, Safeco Field, and the Seattle SuperSonics play basketball at the KeyArena.

In Tacoma you'll find the Northwest Trek, a wildlife park where animals roam freely and can be viewed up close. Bison, bighorn sheep, elk, and mountain goats are just a few of the animals on the trek. The Point Defiance Zoo and Aquarium is one of the top zoos in the country. It is located in Tacoma Washington Park. This 29-acre (12-ha) zoo brings

(opposite)
Deer roam the grassy hills of Olympic National Park.

66

you eye to eye with beluga whales, sharks, and reptiles.

Across Puget Sound is Bremerton, home of the Naval Shipyard Museum. Model ships, weapons, and memorabilia from navy vessels illustrate the history of the United States Navy. At the Naval Undersea Museum in Keyport, visitors can see a large collection of naval undersea objects such as submarines and torpedoes. An exhibit called the Ocean Environment teaches people about the world under the sea with hands-on activities. Outdoors you'll find a submersible that is released underwater to explore depths of 8,000 feet (2,438 m) or more.

In the far western part of Washington is Olympic National Park. This wilderness park measures about 1,429 square miles (3,700 sq km), a little less than half the size of Rhode Island. Olympic National Park seems like three parks, with rugged glacier-capped mountains, more than 60 miles (96 km) of wild Pacific coast, and magnificent old-growth and temperate rain forests. You

can hike to see 300-foot (91-m) trees, towering Mount Olympus, or rarely seen mountain goats. The park is so wild that some areas don't have trails or roads.

Whale watching is a popular summer activity at the San Juan Islands, where orcas swim off the shores. You can only get to the islands by air, boat, or ferry. You can also visit the Whale Museum on San Juan Island. If you prefer the outdoors, some of the most popular bicycling areas in

An orca (killer whale) surfs off the coast of the San Juan Islands.

the Northwest are along the winding country roads of these islands.

Because Native Americans were the first people on Washington's land, we'll end our tour at the Makah Reservation on the northwestern tip of the Olympic Peninsula. In 1970, scientists uncovered an ancient whaling village at Ozette on the Makah Reservation. It is one of the most important archaeological discoveries in North America. By studying artifacts such as tools, weapons, and even furniture, scientists can find out about the history of the Ozette village. Visit the Makah Cultural and Research Center to learn about this great find. You can also see replicas of cedar longhouses and canoes, and learn about the Makah's current whaling efforts.

Wherever you are in Washington, from vast desert areas to dense rain forests to bustling cities, there is plenty to do. The Evergreen State has much to offer in the way of history, culture, entertainment, and natural beauty. Washington has something for everyone.

FIND OUT MORE

Whaling was once a thriving industry. Why did it die out? What impact did it have on the whale population around the world?

WASHINGTON ALMANAC

Statehood date and number: November 11, 1889; 42nd state

State seal: The state seal has a portrait of George Washington with the words "The Seal of the State of Washington, 1889." Adopted in 1889.

State flag: The state flag has a dark green background with the state seal in the center. The flag design was adopted in 1923.

Geographic center: 10 miles (16 km) west-southwest of Wenatchee

Total area/rank: 71,300 square miles (184,665 sq km)/19th

Coastline/rank: 157 miles (253 km)/12th

Borders: British Columbia, Canada; Idaho; Oregon; Pacific Ocean

Longitude and longitude: Washington is located approximately between 47° N and 120° W

Highest/lowest elevation: Mount Rainier, at 14,416 feet (4,397 m)/Pacific Ocean (sea level)

Hottest/coldest temperature: 118° F (48° C) on August 5, 1961, at Ice Harbor Dam/–48° F (–44° C) on December 30, 1968, at Mazama and Winthrop

Land area/rank: 66,544 square miles (172,348 sq km)/20th

Inland water area/rank: 1,553 square miles (4,022 sq km)/11th

Population (2000 Census)/rank: 5,894,121/15th

Population of major cities:

Seattle: 563,374

Spokane: 195,629

Tacoma: 193,556

Vancouver: 143,560

Bellevue: 109,569

Origin of state name: Named for the first United States president, George Washington

State capital: Olympia

Counties: 39

State government: 49 senators, 98 representatives

Major rivers and lakes: Columbia, Snake, Pend Oreille, Spokane, Okanogan, Methow, Wenatchee, Yakima, Lewis, Cowlitz, Skagit, Cedar, Puyallup, Nisqually, Nooksack, Sanpoil/Chelan, Washington, Union, Crescent, Cushman, Quinault, Ozette, Wenatchee, Kachers, Keechelus, Cle Elum, Moses, Soap

Farm products: Apples, potatoes, hay, wheat, cherries, grapes, onions, barley, oats, hops, sugar beets, flower bulbs, apricots

Livestock: Poultry, beef cattle, dairy cattle

Manufactured products: Computer software, aircraft, pulp and paper products, lumber and plywood, aluminum, processed fruits and vegetables, machinery, electronics, beverages, plastic products, ships, transportation equipment

Mining products: Sand, gravel, crushed stone, coal, clay, lead, zinc, limestone, gold, magnesium

Fishing products: Sockeye salmon, pink salmon, king chinook salmon, steelhead trout, smallmouth bass, black bass, smelt, halibut, tuna, oysters, pilchards, white sturgeon

Bird: willow goldfinch

Dance: Square dance

Fish: Steelhead trout

Flower: Coast rhododendron

Folk song: "Roll On, Columbia, Roll On," by Woody Guthrie

Fossil: Columbian mammoth

Fruit: Apple

Gem: Petrified wood

Grass: Bluebunch wheatgrass

Insect: Green darner dragonfly

Motto: *Al-ki* or *Alki* (Native American word meaning "by and by")

Nickname: The Evergreen State

Ship: *Lady Washington*

Song: "Washington, My Home" by Helen Davis

Tartan: Green background (represents forests) with perpendicular bands running through it; blue (represents the lakes, rivers and ocean), white (represents snow-capped mountains), red (represents apples and cherries), yellow (represents wheat and grain crops), and black (represents eruption of Mount St. Helens). Designed in 1988; adopted 1991.

Tree: Western hemlock

Wildlife: Elk, white-tailed deer, mule deer, black bears, mountain goats, cougars, mountain lions, Canada lynx, red foxes, coyotes, killer whales, harbor seals, raccoons, beavers, skunks, minks, otters, squirrels, chipmunks, porcupines, marmots, bobcats, crabs

TIMELINE

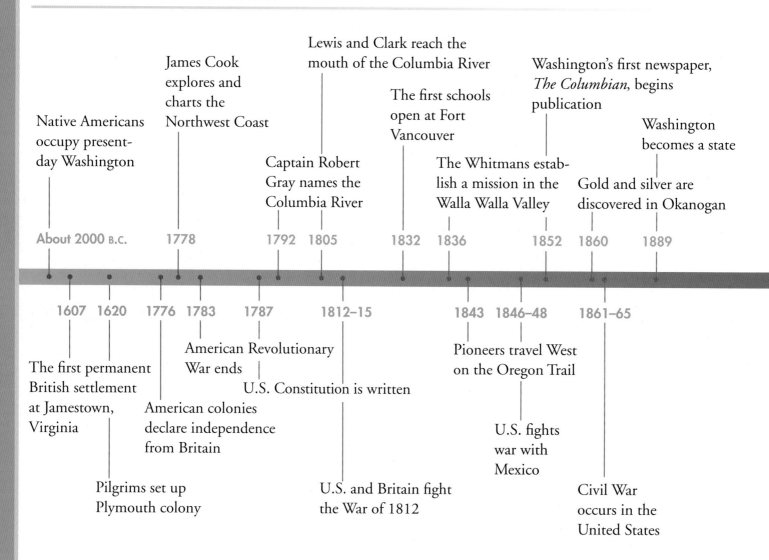

Native Americans occupy present-day Washington

James Cook explores and charts the Northwest Coast

Lewis and Clark reach the mouth of the Columbia River

Captain Robert Gray names the Columbia River

The first schools open at Fort Vancouver

The Whitmans estab-lish a mission in the Walla Walla Valley

Washington's first newspaper, *The Columbian*, begins publication

Gold and silver are discovered in Okanogan

Washington becomes a state

About 2000 B.C.   1778   1792   1805   1832   1836   1852   1860   1889

1607   1620   1776   1783   1787   1812–15   1843   1846–48   1861–65

The first permanent British settlement at Jamestown, Virginia

Pilgrims set up Plymouth colony

American colonies declare independence from Britain

American Revolutionary War ends

U.S. Constitution is written

U.S. and Britain fight the War of 1812

Pioneers travel West on the Oregon Trail

U.S. fights war with Mexico

Civil War occurs in the United States

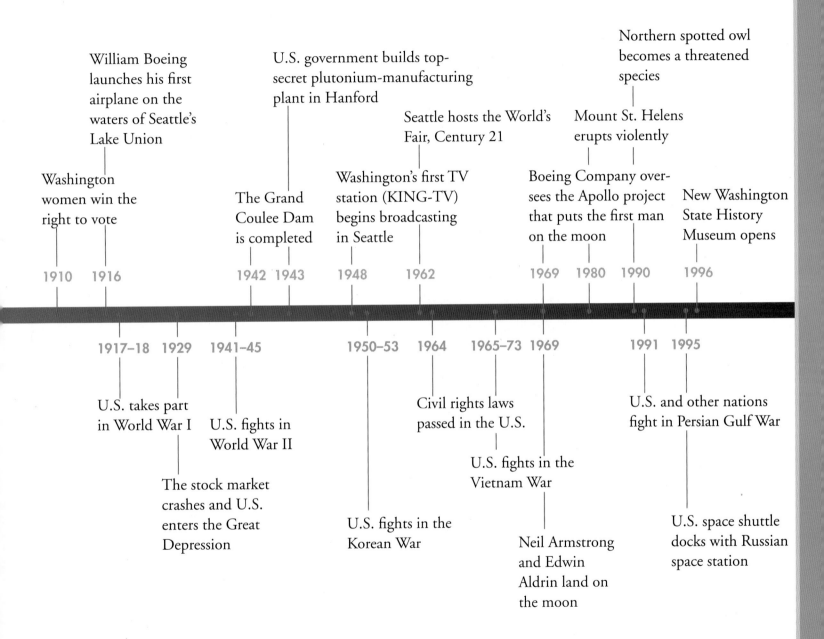

William Boeing launches his first airplane on the waters of Seattle's Lake Union

U.S. government builds top-secret plutonium-manufacturing plant in Hanford

Northern spotted owl becomes a threatened species

Seattle hosts the World's Fair, Century 21

Mount St. Helens erupts violently

Washington women win the right to vote

The Grand Coulee Dam is completed

Washington's first TV station (KING-TV) begins broadcasting in Seattle

Boeing Company over-sees the Apollo project that puts the first man on the moon

New Washington State History Museum opens

1910   1916   1942 1943   1948   1962   1969   1980 1990   1996

1917–18 1929   1941–45   1950–53   1964   1965–73 1969   1991 1995

U.S. takes part in World War I

U.S. fights in World War II

Civil rights laws passed in the U.S.

U.S. and other nations fight in Persian Gulf War

The stock market crashes and U.S. enters the Great Depression

U.S. fights in the Vietnam War

U.S. fights in the Korean War

Neil Armstrong and Edwin Aldrin land on the moon

U.S. space shuttle docks with Russian space station

GALLERY OF FAMOUS WASHINGTONIANS

Chester F. Carlson
(1906–1968)
Invented xerography, the copying process to reproduce images, known today as photocopying. Born in Seattle.

Bing Crosby (Harry Lillis Crosby)
(1903–1977)
Academy Award-winning singer and actor. He made more than 55 feature films and recorded more than 1,700 songs during his career, including the best seller, "White Christmas." Born in Tacoma.

John Elway
(1960–)
Quarterback for the Denver Broncos until 1999. Elway led the Broncos to the Super Bowl in 1987 and 1988. Born in Port Angeles.

Richard Gordon, Jr.
(1929–)
Astronaut who piloted the *Gemini XI* spacecraft around Earth in 1966. In 1969 he flew the *Apollo XII* spacecraft for the second landing on the moon. Born in Seattle.

Carolyn Kizer
(1925–)
Poet and founder of *Poetry Northwest* magazine. Kizer won the Pulitzer Prize for her collection of poetry called *Yin: New Poems*. Born in Spokane.

Gary Larson
(1950–)
Cartoonist. Larson created the comic strip "The Far Side." Born in Tacoma.

Betty MacDonald
(1908–1958)
Well-known author of the Mrs. Piggle-Wiggle books and several other titles. Lived on Vashon Island.

Dixie Lee Ray
(1914–1994)
Zoologist at the University of Washington and chairperson of the U.S. Atomic Energy Commission. Ray became the first female governor (1977–1981) in Washington State. Born in Tacoma.

Dick Scobee
(1939–1986)
Famous astronaut. Scobee died January 28, 1986, when the space shuttle *Challenger* exploded shortly after liftoff from the Kennedy Space Center in Florida. Born in Cle Elum.

Minoru Yamasaki
(1912–1986)
American architect. Most famous for designing the World Trade Center in New York City, which is no longer standing. Born in Seattle.

GLOSSARY

ancient: belonging to a time long ago

antique: a valuable object from the past

artificial: made by humans; not natural

astronomy: the study of planets, stars, and other heavenly bodies

conservation: the protection and careful management of something so it won't be wasted

constitution: the basic rules and principles by which a country, town, or organization is run

dormant: a term used to describe a volcano that is presently inactive but which may erupt again

engineer: a person who uses science and math to design useful things such as roads and buildings

erosion: the gradual wearing away of land by water, wind, or glaciers

expedition: a trip for a certain purpose such as an exploration

gorge: a deep, narrow valley

hydroelectricity: electric power that is produced by flowing water

irrigation: bringing water to an area of land using ditches, pipes, or sprinklers

isolated: separated from others

legislature: a group of people with the duty to make laws for a country, state, or province

loess: deposits of fine soil transported by the wind

manufacture: the process of making something

merchant: a person who buys and sells things for profit

missionary: a person who travels to faraway places in order to do religious or charitable work

monorail: a single rail used as a track for wheeled vehicles such as trains or cars that are balanced or suspended from it

perpendicular: a surface forming a right angle with another surface

plateau: an elevated, flat area of land

population: the number of people in a city or country

reservation: land that is set aside for Native Americans

settlement: place where a permanent community has been set up

transcontinental: crossing the continent

treaty: an agreement between nations or groups

tributary: a stream that flows into a larger stream

FOR MORE INFORMATION

Web sites

State of Washington Web site
http://access.wa.gov
Official Web site for the Washington State government.

Washington State Legislature Kids' Page
http://www.leg.wa.gov/legislature/StudentsPage
Links to everything you need to know about the government of Washington State. Test your knowledge with a fun trivia contest.

Washington State Library
http://www.secstate.wa.gov/library
Contains information about Washington and its government.

Washington State Tourism
http://www.experiencewashington.com
Contains information about things to do and see in Washington. Useful for help on geography homework about Washington.

Books

Blackwood, Gary L. *Life on the Oregon Trail*. San Diego, CA: Lucent Books, 1999.

Lauber, Patricia. *Volcano: The Eruption and Healing of Mount St. Helens*. New York, NY: Simon & Schuster Books for Young Readers, 1986.

Oyawin Eder, Jeanne M. *The Makah*. New York, NY: Raintree/Steck Vaughn, 2000.

Stein, Conrad R. *Seattle*. Danbury, CT: Children's Press, 1999.

Addresses

Washington State Historical Society
1911 Pacific Avenue
Tacoma, WA 98402

Washington State Capitol Campus
P. O. Box 41000
Olympia, WA 98504-1000

INDEX

ABOUT THE AUTHOR

Christine Webster is a children's book author with a special interest in United States history. Her work for Children's Press includes books in the From Sea to Shining Sea and Cornerstones of Freedom series, including *The Pledge of Allegiance* and *Lewis and Clark*. She lives in Canada with her husband and three children.